Hot Math Topics

Problem Solving, Communication, and Reasoning

About Money and Time

grade 1

Carole Greenes
Linda Schulman Dacey
Rika Spungin

Dale Seymour Publications®
Parsippany, New Jersey

This book is published by Dale Seymour Publications®,
an imprint of Pearson Learning.

Dale Seymour Publications
299 Jefferson Road
Parsippany, New Jersey 07054-0480
Customer Service: 800-872-1100

Editorial Manager: Carolyn Coyle
Project Editor: Mali Apple
Production/Manufacturing Director: Janet Yearian
Production/Manufacturing Manager: Karen Edmonds
Production/Manufacturing Coordinator: Lorraine Allen
Design Director: Phyllis Aycock
Text and Cover Design: Tracey Munz
Cover and Interior Illustrations: Jared Lee
Computer Graphics: Alan Noyes

Copyright © 2001 by Dale Seymour Publications®.
All rights reserved.
Printed in the United States of America.

The publisher grants permission to individual teachers who have purchased this book to reproduce the blackline masters as needed for use with their own students. Reproduction for an entire school or school district or for commercial use is prohibited.

Order number 27500
ISBN 0-7690-0830-5

1 2 3 4 5 6 7 8 9 10-ML-04 03 02 01 00

This Book Is Printed
On Recycled Paper

contents

Introduction 1

Management Chart 6

Award Certificate 6

Problems and Tasks 7

    Money Problems and Tasks 8

    Time Problems and Tasks 38

Answers 58

Introduction

Why Was *Hot Math Topics* Developed?

The *Hot Math Topics* series was developed for several reasons:

- to offer children practice and maintenance of previously learned skills and concepts
- to enhance problem solving and mathematical reasoning abilities
- to build literacy skills
- to nurture collaborative learning behaviors

Practicing and maintaining concepts and skills

Although textbooks and core curriculum materials do treat the topics explored in this series, their treatment is often limited by the lesson format and the page size. As a consequence, there are often not enough opportunities for children to practice newly acquired concepts and skills related to the topics, or to connect the topics to other content areas. *Hot Math Topics* provides the necessary practice and mathematical connections.

Similarly, core instructional programs often do not do a very good job of helping children maintain their skills. Although textbooks do include reviews of previously learned material, they are often limited to sidebars or boxed-off areas on one or two pages in each chapter, with four or five exercises in each box. Each set of problems is intended only as a sampling of previously taught topics, rather than as a complete review. In the selection and placement of the review exercises, little or no attention is given to levels of complexity of the problems. By contrast, *Hot Math Topics* targets specific topics and gives children more experience with concepts and skills related to them. The problems are sequenced by difficulty, allowing children to hone their skills. And, because they are not tied to specific lessons, the problems can be used at any time.

Enhancing problem solving and mathematical reasoning abilities

Hot Math Topics present children with situations in which they may use a variety of problem solving strategies, including

- designing and conducting experiments to generate or collect data
- guessing, checking, and revising guesses
- organizing data in lists or tables in order to identify patterns and relationships
- choosing appropriate computational algorithms and deciding on a sequence of computations
- using inverse operations in "work backward" solution paths

For their solutions, children are also required to bring to bear various methods of reasoning, including

- deductive reasoning
- inductive reasoning
- proportional reasoning

For example, to solve clue-type problems, children must reason deductively and make inferences about mathematical relationships in order to generate candidates for the solutions and to home in on those that meet all of the problem's conditions.

To identify and continue a pattern and then verbalize a rule for finding the next term in that pattern, children must reason inductively.

To compute unit prices and make trades, children must reason proportionally.

To estimate or compare magnitudes of numbers, or to determine the type of number appropriate for a given situation, children must apply their number sense skills.

Building communication and literacy skills

Hot Math Topics offers children opportunities to write and talk about mathematical ideas. For many problems, children must describe their solution paths, justify their solutions, give their opinions, or write or tell stories.

Some problems have multiple solution methods. With these problems, children may have to compare their methods with those of their peers and talk about how their approaches are alike and different.

Other problems have multiple solutions, requiring children to confer to be sure they have found all possible answers.

Nurturing collaborative learning behaviors

Several of the problems can be solved by children working together. Some are designed specifically as partner problems. By working collaboratively, children can develop expertise in posing questions that call for clarification or verification, brainstorming solution strategies, and following another person's line of reasoning.

What Is in *About Money and Time*?

This book contains 100 problems and tasks, 60 about money and 40 about time. The mathematics content, the mathematical connections, the problem solving strategies, and the communication skills that are emphasized are described below.

Mathematics content

Money problems and tasks require children to

- identify coins and their values
- identify values of sets of coins
- compare values of sets of coins
- construct different sets of coins with the same value
- share and combine collections of coins
- compute with amounts of money less than one dollar and with whole-dollar amounts

Time problems and tasks require children to

- tell and show time to the hour and half hour on analog and digital clocks
- order events temporally
- match events to amounts of time
- estimate and compute elapsed time
- create and complete schedules
- identify days and dates on calendars

Mathematical connections

In these problems and tasks, connections are made to these other topic areas:

- arithmetic
- algebra
- graphs
- number sense

Problem solving strategies

About Money and Time problems and tasks offer children opportunities to use one or more of several problem solving strategies.

- **Formulate Questions:** When data are presented in displays or text form, children must pose one or more questions that can be answered using the given data.

- **Complete Stories:** When confronted with an incomplete story, children must supply the missing information and then check that the story makes sense.

- **Organize Information:** To ensure that several solution candidates for a problem are considered, children may have to organize information by drawing a picture, making a list, or completing a table.

- **Guess, Check, and Revise:** In some problems, children have to identify or generate candidates for the solution and then check whether those candidates match the conditions of the problem. If the conditions are not satisfied, other possible solutions must be generated and verified.

- **Identify and Continue Patterns:** To identify the next term or terms in a sequence, children have to recognize the relationship between successive terms and then generalize that relationship.

- **Use Logic:** Children have to reason deductively, from clues, to make inferences about the solution to a problem. They have to reason inductively to continue numeric patterns.

- **Work Backward:** In some problems, the output is given and children must determine the input by identifying mathematical relationships between the input and output and applying inverse operations.

Communication skills

Problems and tasks in *About Money and Time* are designed to stimulate communication. As part of the solution process, children may have to

- describe their thinking
- find alternate solution methods and solution paths
- identify other possible answers
- formulate problems for classmates to solve
- compare solutions and methods with classmates
- explain mathematical ideas

These communication skills are enhanced when children interact with one another and with the teacher. By communicating both orally and in writing, children develop their understanding and use of the language of mathematics.

How Can *Hot Math Topics* Be Used?

The problems may be used as practice of newly learned concepts and skills, as maintenance of previously learned ideas, and as enrichment experiences for early finishers or more advanced students.

They may be used in class or given to children to take home and do with their families. If used during class, they may be selected to complement lessons dealing with a specific topic or assigned every week as a means of keeping skills alive and well. For children whom the reading requirements of the problems exceed their current abilities, you may wish to use the problems in whole-class or group settings, where either you or an able reader presents the problems aloud.

As they become more able readers, children can work on the problems in pairs or on their own. The problems are sequenced from least to most difficult. The selection of problems may be made by the teacher or the children based on their needs or interests. If the plan is for children to choose problems, you may wish to copy individual problems onto card stock and laminate them, and establish a problem card file.

To facilitate record keeping, a Management Chart is provided on page 6. The chart can be duplicated so that there is one for each child. As a problem is completed, the space corresponding to that problem's number may be shaded. An Award Certificate is included on page 6 as well.

How Can Children's Performance Be Assessed?

About Money and Time problems and tasks provide you with opportunities to assess children's

- knowledge of money and time
- problem solving abilities
- mathematical reasoning methods
- communication skills

Observations

Keeping anecdotal records helps you to remember important information you gain as you observe children at work. To make observations more manageable, limit each observation to a group of from four to six children or to one of the areas noted above. You may find that using index cards facilitates the recording process.

Discussions

Many of the *About Money and Time* problems and tasks allow for multiple answers or may be solved in a variety of ways. This built-in richness motivates children to discuss their work with one another. Small groups or class discussions are appropriate. As children share their approaches to the problems, you will gain additional insights into their content knowledge, mathematical reasoning, and communication abilities.

Scoring responses

You may wish to holistically score children's responses to the problems and tasks. The simple scoring rubric below uses three levels: high, medium, and low.

Portfolios

Having children store their responses to the problems in *Hot Math Topics* portfolios allows them to see improvement in their work over time. You may want to have them choose examples of their best responses for inclusion in their permanent portfolios, accompanied by explanations as to why each was chosen.

High	Medium	Low
• Solution demonstrates that the child knows the concepts and skills.	• Solution demonstrates that the child has some knowledge of the concepts and skills.	• Solution shows that the child has little or no grasp of the concepts and skills.
• Solution is complete and thorough.	• Solution is complete.	• Solution is incomplete or contains major errors.
• The child communicates effectively.	• The child communicates somewhat clearly.	• The child does not communicate effectively.

Children and the assessment process

Involving children in the assessment process is central to the development of their abilities to reflect on their own work, to understand the assessment standards to which they are held accountable, and to take ownership for their own learning. Young children may find the reflective process difficult, but with your coaching, they can develop such skills.

Discussion may be needed to help children better understand your standards for performance. Ask children such questions as, "What does it mean to communicate *clearly*?" "What is a *complete* response?" Some children may want to use the high-medium-low rubric to score their responses. Others may prefer to use a simple visual evaluation, such as these characters:

Participation in peer-assessment tasks will also help children to better understand the performance standards. In pairs or small groups, children can review each other's responses and offer feedback. Opportunities to revise work may then be given.

What Additional Materials Are Needed?

Jump ropes, minute timers, cups, number cubes, and play money (pennies, dimes, nickels, and quarters) are required for some of the tasks. Other measurement devices and manipulative materials, although not required, may be useful for some children: a clock face or real analog and digital clocks, play money (bills), and calendars. Colored pencils or crayons should be readily accessible. Calculators are not required for any of the tasks, although some children may find them beneficial.

Management Chart

Name _____

When a problem or task is completed, shade the box with that number.

1	2	3	4	5	6	7	8	9	10
11	12	13	14	15	16	17	18	19	20
21	22	23	24	25	26	27	28	29	30
31	32	33	34	35	36	37	38	39	40
41	42	43	44	45	46	47	48	49	50
51	52	53	54	55	56	57	58	59	60
61	62	63	64	65	66	67	68	69	70
71	72	73	74	75	76	77	78	79	80
81	82	83	84	85	86	87	88	89	90
91	92	93	94	95	96	97	98	99	100

Award Certificate

Hot Math Topics

SUPER SOLVER

this certifies that

_____

has been awarded the Hot Math Topics Super Solver Certificate for

Excellence in Problem Solving

_____ _____
date   signature

Problems and Tasks

How much does each design cost?

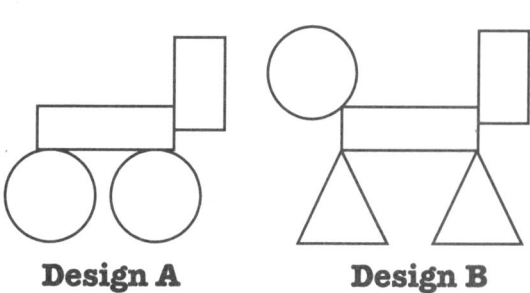

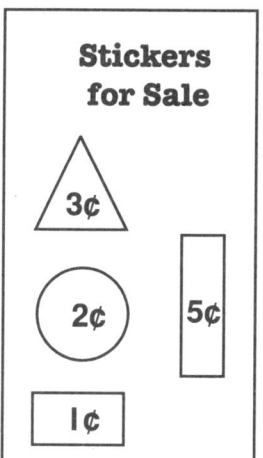

Design A   Design B

Work with a friend.

Draw a new design with the stickers.

Have your friend tell the cost.

Get a cup of pennies.

Take out a handful of pennies.

Tell how many cents you have.

What other coins would make the same amount of money?

Make a list.

Write a story problem for the picture.

Give the answer to your problem.

- -

Mario spent a dime.

He bought a star sticker and a rainbow sticker.

What other sticker did he buy?

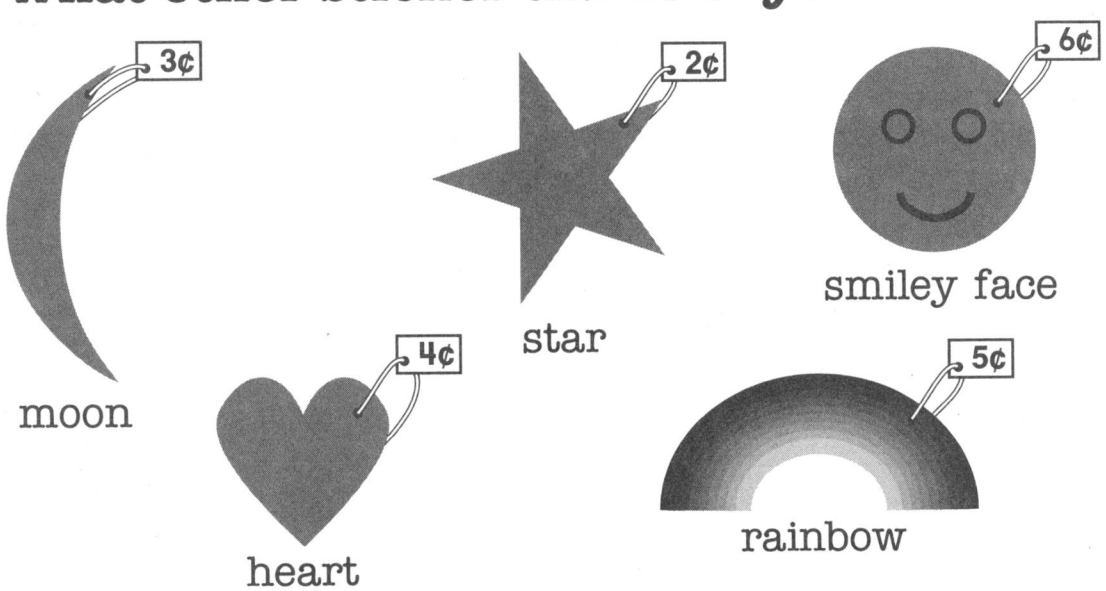

Work with a friend. ⑤
- Close your eyes.
- Have your friend put a coin in your hand.
- Tell the coin.
- Take turns and try again.

Talk about how you can tell the coins.

Fill in the blanks with numbers. ⑥
The story must make sense.

Max has _____ ¢.

He bought a pencil for _____ ¢.

He has _____ ¢ left.

You had  .

You earned  .

How much money do you have now?

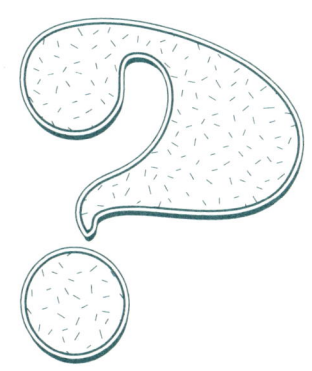

Play with a friend. Take turns.

On each turn

- Roll a number cube.
- Take that number of pennies.
- Trade for nickels or dimes if you can.

The first player to get 5 dimes is the winner!

About Money and Time 11

Who has more money?
Tell how you know.

Patricia's money:

Julian's money:

- -

Write P, N, or D in each circle.

- Every row must have

- Every column must have

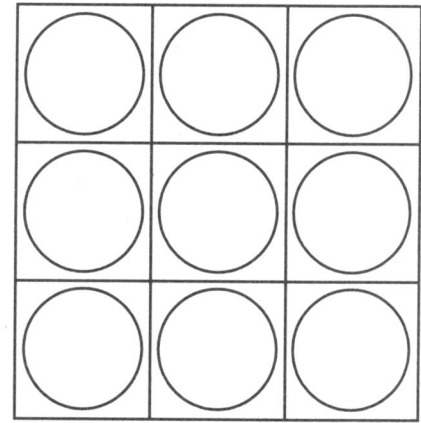

How much money is in each row?

Who has the most money? Who has the least money?

Ari's money:

Ben's money:

Cal's money:

Use dimes, nickels, or pennies. List the other ways to make 13¢.

Dimes	Nickels	Pennies
0	2	3

About Money and Time

How much is the bracelet?

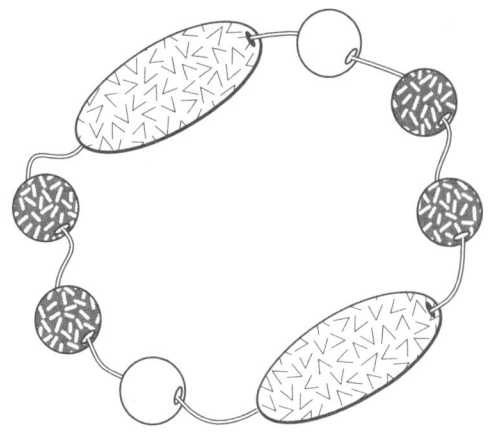

Use the beads.
Draw another bracelet.
Tell how much it costs.

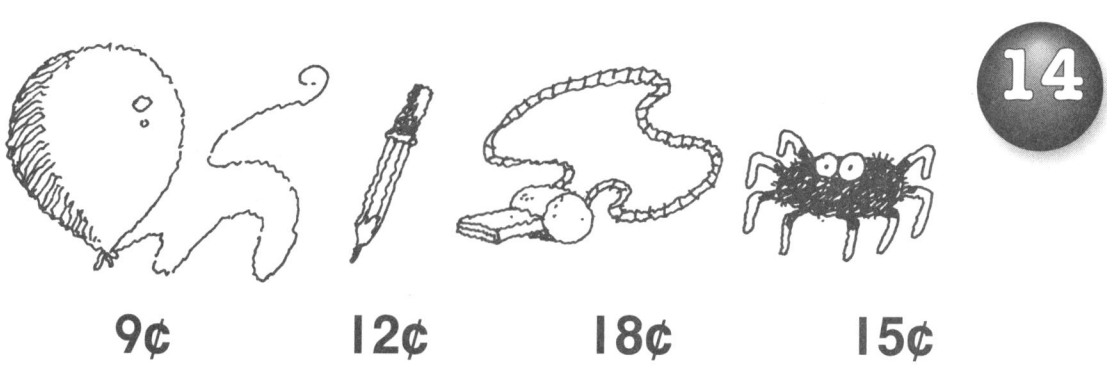

9¢   12¢   18¢   15¢

You have  .

Which 2 different toys could you buy?

Write a problem about these bags of coins.

Bag A

Bag Z

Answer your problem.

Give it to a friend to solve.

Spend 25¢ on stickers.

Make a list of stickers you could buy.

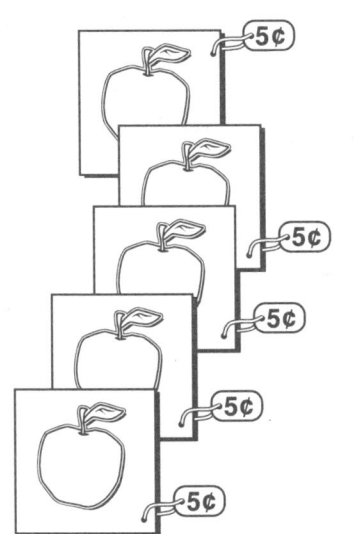
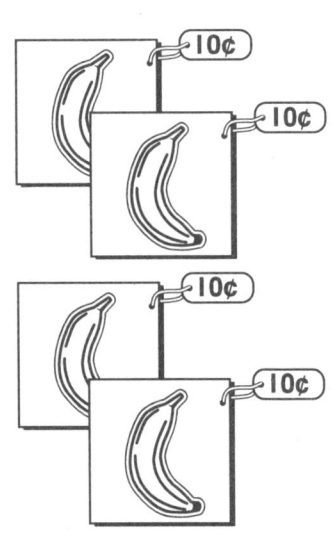

About Money and Time

17

You have ⓘⓘⓘⓘⓘⓘ.

Spend all of your money.

You can buy more than one of each toy.

What will you buy?

18

How can you spend exactly 15¢ at the yard sale?

Tell another way.

Amy has 2 dimes and 6 pennies.
Olga has 1 dime and 2 nickels.
Who has more money?
How much more?

The chart shows how much money each friend has.

Name	Money
Abe	 2 dimes, 3 pennies
Kate	 1 quarter
Yumi	 1 nickel, 1 dime, 1 penny
Arnon	 3 nickels, 5 pennies

Yumi has more money than Abe.
How much more?

About Money and Time

How much money does Mai Lin have?

Choose an answer from the sign.

- She has less than a quarter.
- She has no pennies.

Tell how you know.

How much do 3 stickers cost?

Tell how you know.

Shakara has these coins:

She wants to buy the apple juice.

How much more money does she need?

You have 22¢.

How many baseball cards can you buy?

Baseball Cards 5¢ each

Play with a friend.

Put these coins in a bag:

Hide 3 of the coins in your hand.

Tell your friend how much money you have.

Have your friend name the coins.

How much does each toy cost?

- The train costs the most.
- The car does not cost the least.

The car costs _____.

The boat costs _____.

The train costs _____.

Toy Prices
$5 $8 $11

Which is Greg's: A, B, C, or D?

- He has 4 coins.
- He has no dimes.
- He has more than 10¢.

How much money does Greg have?

A B C D

Use the numbers on the sign.
The story must make sense.

- The skates cost the most.
  They cost $____.
- The helmet costs $7 less than the shoes.
  The helmet costs $____.
- The shoes cost $____.

12   5
   20

Lea has these coins:

Which book can she buy?

Todd's money: Ang's money:

Todd gave money to Ang.
Now they have the same amount.
How much did Todd give to Ang?

You have some money.
- You spend 13¢.
- You have 15¢ left.

How much money did you have to start?

Show this money with 4 coins.

31

The pattern continues.
There are 10 coins.

32

How much money is there?

About Money and Time

33

Jenna wants to buy the kite.
She has 30¢.
Brad gave her these coins:

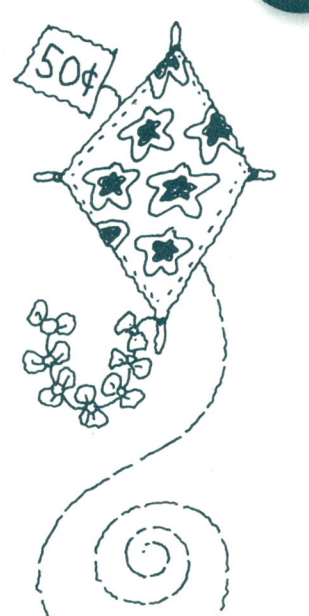

How much more money does she need?

34

Batai and Lehie share this money:

How much does each friend get?

 =

*	*	*	*
*	*	*	*

= _____ ¢

- -

36

Nickels   **Dimes**

Which is more money?

the stack   the stack
of nickels   **or**   of dimes

Tell two ways to know.

About Money and Time **25**

How much money do I have?

- I have less than 40¢.
- I don't have any pennies.
- I have more than 2 dimes.
- I have 1 nickel.

Which costs more, X or Y?
Tell two ways to know.

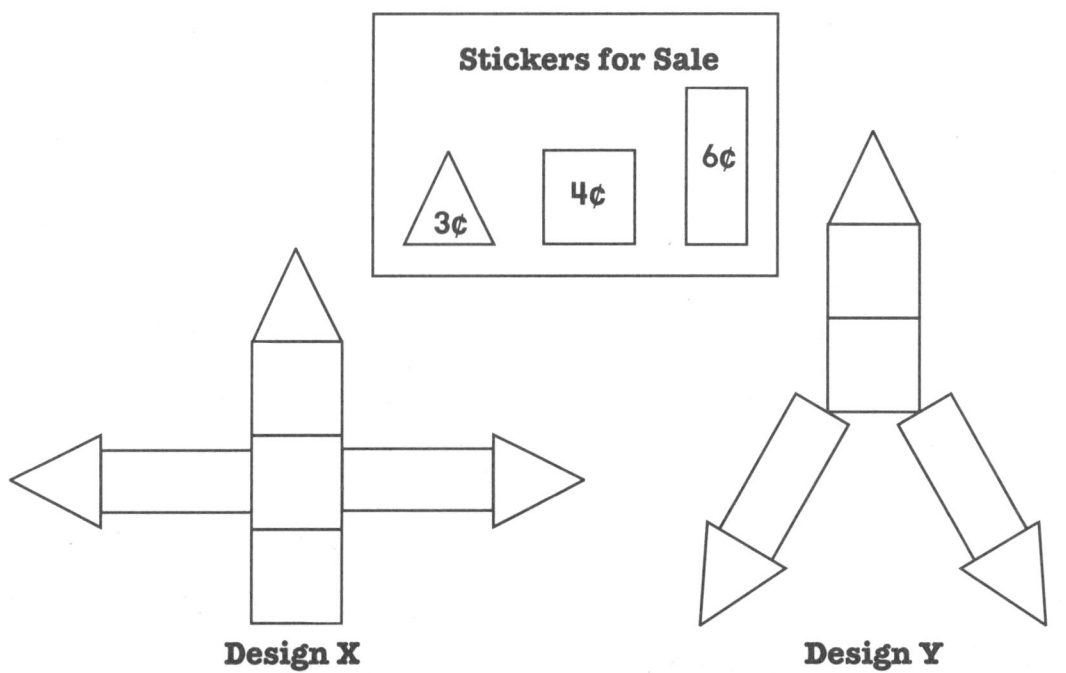

Draw lines. Match each person to the coins. 〔39〕

Kara: "I have more than 1 dollar."

José: "I have less than Ana."

Ana: "I have 52¢."

Fill in the blanks. 〔40〕

The story must make sense.

Jan has _____ ¢.

Mike has _____ ¢.

Jan has _____ ¢ more than Mike.

Together they have _____ ¢.

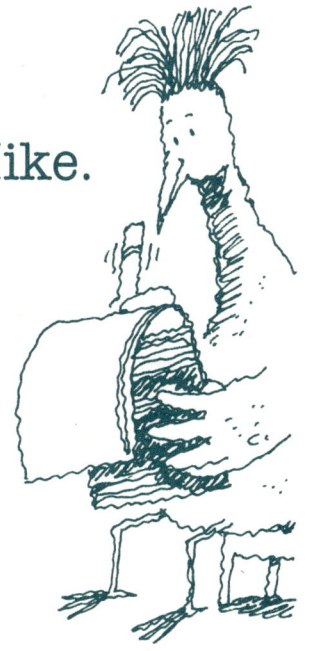

About Money and Time

41

Mateo has these coins in his left hand:

He has the same coins in his right hand.

How much money does he have in all?

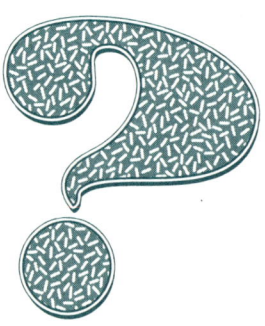

42

You have these coins:

How many bows can you buy?

Your friend gives you pennies.
- On day 1, you get 1 penny.
- On day 2, you get 3 pennies.
- On day 3, you get 5 pennies.
- On day 4, you get 7 pennies.

On what day will you get 15¢?

You have 2 dimes and 4 nickels.

Put 1 coin in each circle.

The 3 coins on each side of the triangle must add to 20¢.

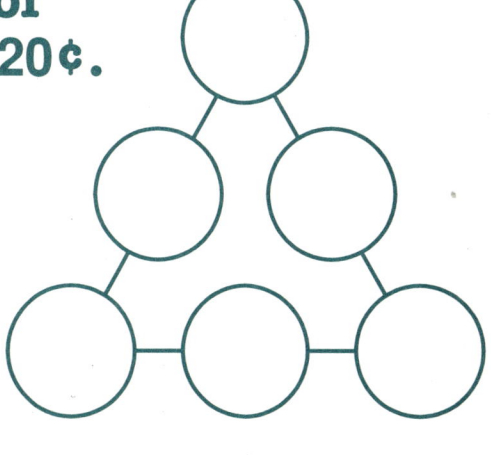

45

You have 30¢.

Can you buy more 3¢ stamps or more 2¢ stamps?

How many more?

46

Darnell gave half of his money to Lana.

Here are the coins he gave Lana:

How much money did Darnell have at the start?

Rico had    .

He bought one of these things.

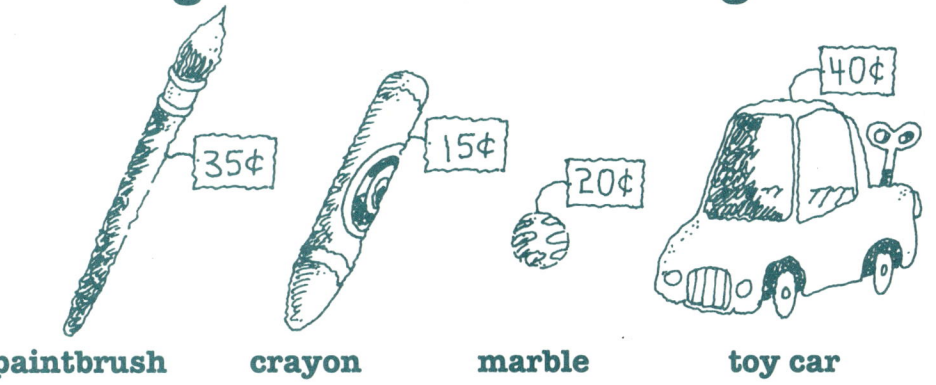

paintbrush   crayon   marble   toy car

Now he has   . **What did he buy?**

Dana has 3 coins.

- She has less than 25¢.
- She does not have any pennies.

What coins could she have?

Zoe's money:

Sam's money:

49

Who has more money?

How much more?

Lelia has 50¢ in quarters, nickels, and dimes.

50

What coins does Lelia have?

She has _____ quarter.

She has _____ dime.

She has _____ nickels.

Linda has 10¢ more than Rita.
Carl has 25¢ less than Linda.
Who has the most money?
Tell how you know.

---

25   4   12   1

Use the numbers shown.
The story must make sense.

Aleta has ____¢.

Aleta has ____ coin.

Joshua has ____¢.

Joshua has ____ coins.

What coins does Joshua have?

Which bank has more dimes? How do you know?

The piggy bank has 23¢.

The duck bank has 26¢.

Buy a lemonade. What coins could you use? Show two other ways.

Mr. Clark spent $34.

- He bought a T-shirt for each of his children.
- He bought a cap for himself.

How many children does he have?

Denis, Lydia, and Hana share this money.

They each get the same amount of money.

How much will each get?

Tell how you decided.

57

The pattern continues.
There are 15 coins.
How much money is there?

58

The bag holds 2 bills and 1 coin.
What is in the bag?

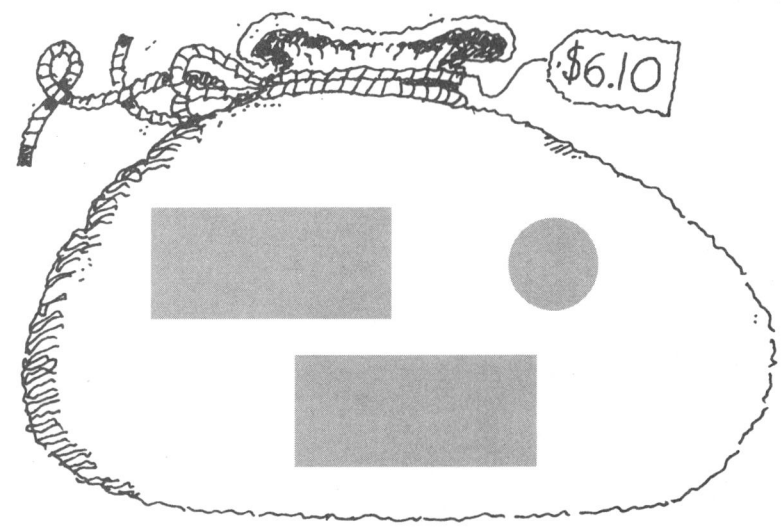

What should Tanya tell Karen?

There is 1 quarter in each box.
There are 3 nickels in each can.
Do you want the boxes or the cans?
Tell why.

**Put the pictures in order.
Tell a story.
Write 1, 2, 3, 4.**

Name 2 things you do in the morning.

Name 2 things you do in the afternoon.

Name 2 things you do in the evening.

Which clock shows the time I go to school?

- It is before 9:00.
- It is after 7:30.
- It is not 8:30.

2 hours   1 minute   10 minutes

Which time above is closest to

- the time it takes to color a picture? _____
- the time it takes to write your name and address? _____
- the time it takes to watch a movie? _____

There are 31 days in August.

On this calendar, what day is the last day of the month?

S	M	T	W	T	F	S
		1	2	3	4	5	6

August

Make a life line.

- Think of something important that happened each year.
- Draw a picture for each year.
- Tape the pictures together to make a life line.

Compare your life line with a friend's life line.

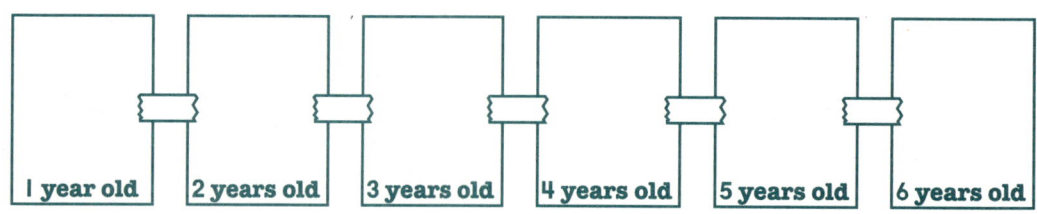

Tell something that takes less time than
- making your bed: _____
- eating dinner: _____
- sleeping at night: _____

The clocks show afternoon times.

Write the times in order from earliest to latest.

_____ _____ _____ _____ _____

earliest   **latest**

Which month is your favorite?

_____

Draw a picture to show why you like that month.

The class had a party.

- It was between December 6 and December 12.
- It was after Monday.
- It was before Thursday.
- It was not Tuesday.

S	M	T	W	T	F	S
	1	2	3	4	5	6
7	8	9	10	11	12	13
14	15	16	17	18	19	20
21	22	23	24	25	26	27
28	29	30	31			

December

Find the date and the day of the week.

Pia wants to watch a movie that is 2 hours long.

She has to go to bed at 8:30.

Does she have time to watch the movie?

Tell how you know.

Jon has breakfast at 8:30.

His music lesson starts an hour later.

It lasts 30 minutes.

Show the time Jon's music lesson is over.

The chart shows how many children go to bed at each time.

7:00	♀♀
7:30	♀♀♀♀♀♀♀♀♀♀♀♀
8:00	♀♀♀♀♀♀♀♀♀
8:30	♀♀♀♀

How many children don't go to bed at 7:30?

Put the pictures in order.

Tell a story.

Write 1, 2, 3, 4.

Which takes more time?

Count to 50.   Snap your fingers 20 times.

How did you decide?

The soccer game starts at 9:30.

The soccer game ends 2 hours later.

Show the end time on the clock.

SPRING SUMMER WINTER FALL

Which season do you like best?

Tell 3 things you like to do in this season.

Seth's vacation starts on March 17.

It is 2 weeks long.

Miki's vacation starts on March 12 and ends on March 28.

Whose vacation is longer?

How much longer?

Today is Thursday, July 15.
I go to camp in 10 days.
On what day do I go to camp?
Tell how you know.

Ask 10 friends what time they go to bed.

Make a list of their answers.

How many friends go to bed

- before you do?
- after you do?
- at the same time you do?

Times

Use the numbers shown.

The story must make sense.

Sol is ____ years old.

In 1 year he will be ____ years old.

His brother is ____ years old.

His mother is ____ years old.

I fell down the day before yesterday.

Today is Monday.

On what day did I fall down?

**Tamara came to the race at 4:00.
She was a half hour late.
What time did the race start?**

**Write the time under each clock.
Then write 2 things you can do at each time.**

Morning   Afternoon   Night

_____ _____ _____

_____ _____ _____

_____ _____ _____

Tanya's birthday is July 22.

Kai's birthday is 5 days before Tanya's.

Jason's birthday is 1 week after Kai's.

What is the date of Jason's birthday?

Use the numbers and times on the sign.

Put one in each blank.

The story must make sense.

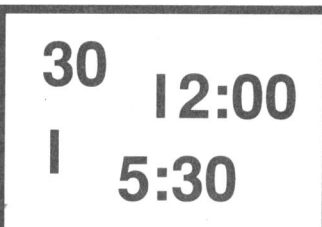

Margot had lunch at _____ .

After lunch she read a book for _____ minutes.

Then she cleaned her room for _____ hour.

At _____ she had dinner.

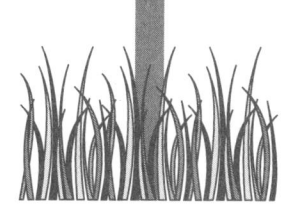

Put these in order.
Write a number on each line.

1 = takes the least time   4 = takes the most time

_____ **Brush your teeth.**
_____ **Grow 2 inches.**
_____ **Read a book.**
_____ **Hop 3 times.**

The date is 10 days *before* April 17.
What is the date? _____

The date is 1 week *after* June 1.
What is the date? _____

What is the date?

Make up two "What is the date?" questions.

Use the word *before* or *after*.

Have a friend answer your questions.

About Money and Time 51

89

Write a story.
Use all the animals.
Use all the times.

Animals	Times
	12:00
	3:30
	4:00

bird

snake

squirrel

90

Fill in the train times.

The train stops at
- Akron at 1 o'clock.
- Kent 1 hour later.
- Eaton 30 minutes later.
- Troy half an hour later.
- Hart at 5 o'clock.

Train Schedule

Stop	Time
Akron	1:00
Kent	
Eaton	
Troy	
Hart	

Who is older?

How many days older?

How many weeks older?

I was 6 years old on May 15.

I was 6 years old on May 1.

Pick one activity to try.

How many times can you do it in 1 minute?

Guess. Then do it.

- jump rope
- snap your fingers
- do jumping jacks

About Money and Time

Draw the hands to show the time you wake up.

Draw the hands to show the time you go to bed.

How much time is it from when you wake up to bedtime?

My Perfect Day!

Pick times of the day.
Write the times.
Tell what you will do at those times.

8:30   2   4   12:30

95

Use the numbers shown.

The story must make sense.

Langston went to camp at _____ .

He came home _____ hours later, at _____ .

Then he played with his brother for _____ hours.

Talk with a friend.

96

How do 3 o'clock and 9 o'clock look alike?

How do they look different?

About Money and Time **55**

97

Make two lists.

Tell what you can do in 1 minute.	Tell what you can do in 1 hour.

I can do 15 pull-ups in 1 minute.

98

piano lesson starts

piano lesson ends

ball game starts

ball game ends

The ball game is longer than the piano lesson. How much longer?

	July					
S	M	T	W	T	F	S
		1	2	3	4	5
6	7	8	9	10	11	12
13	14	15	16	17	18	19
20	21	22	23	24	25	26
27	28	29	30	31		

The calendar shows July.

Which day of the week is August 11?

When are the birthdays?

- Nigel's birthday is in June.
- Tina's birthday is 2 months after Nigel's.
- Theo's birthday is 3 months after Tina's.

Write the month under each person.

_____   _____   _____

Answers

1. 10¢, 14¢; Designs will vary.
2. Answers will vary.
3. Problems will vary.
4. a moon sticker
6. Stories will vary.
7. 45¢
9. Patricia; Explanations will vary.
10. Possible grid: Each row will have 16¢.

P	N	D
D	P	N
N	D	P

11. most, Cal; least, Ben
12.

D	N	P
0	2	3
1	0	3
0	1	8
0	0	13

13. 42¢; Drawings and amounts will vary.
14. balloon and whistle *or* pencil and spider
15. Problems will vary.
16. 2 bananas, 1 apple; 1 banana, 3 apples; 5 apples
17. Possible answers: 5 spiders; 1 spider and 1 snake; 4 spiders and 1 lizard; 2 spiders and 2 lizards; 2 spiders and 1 frog; *or* 1 lizard and 1 frog
18. Possible answers: book and truck *or* 3 books *or* book, ball, and puzzle
19. Amy, 6¢ more
20. 13¢ more
21. 15¢; Explanations will vary.
22. 6¢; Possible explanation: 3 is half of 6, and half of 12¢ is 6¢.
23. 5¢
24. 4 cards
26. $8, $5, $11
27. B, 12¢
28. $20, $5, $12
29. *Plants*
30. 5¢
31. 28¢; 1 quarter and 3 pennies
32. 30¢
33. 3¢
34. 22¢
35. 40¢
36. The stack of dimes. Possible explanations: There is 50¢ in dimes and 40¢ in nickels. *Or* each dime is worth 2 nickels, so the stack of dimes could be replaced by 10 nickels, which is more than are in the stack of nickels.
37. 35¢
38. X; Possible explanation: X has one more square than Y, and all the other shapes are the same.
39. Kara: 2 quarters, 6 dimes; José: 1 dime, 7 nickels, 2 pennies; Ana: 4 dimes, 2 nickels, 2 pennies
40. Stories will vary.
41. 52¢
42. 3 bows

43. day 8
44. Possible arrangement:

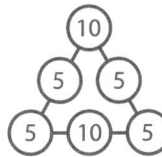

45. more 2¢ stamps, 5 more
46. 44¢
47. the marble
48. 3 nickels *or* 2 nickels and 1 dime
49. Sam, 7¢ more
50. 1, 1, 3
51. Linda; Explanations will vary.
52. 25¢, 1, 12¢, 4; 2 nickels and 2 pennies
53. The duck bank. Possible explanation: Neither bank can have quarters, and the duck bank has more money with fewer coins, so it must have more dimes.
54. Possible answers: 1 half dollar and 1 nickel *or* 2 quarters and 1 nickel *or* 1 quarter and 3 dimes *or* 1 quarter, 2 dimes, and 2 nickels *or* 1 quarter, 1 dime, and 4 nickels *or* 5 dimes and 1 nickel *or* 4 dimes and 3 nickels *or* 3 dimes and 5 nickels *or* 2 dimes and 7 nickels *or* 1 dime and 9 nickels *or* 11 nickels
55. 3 children
56. 22¢; Explanations will vary.
57. $1.00
58. $5 bill, $1 bill, and a dime
59. Answers will vary but should consider the values of the coins as well as the number of coins; Tanya has 3¢ more.

60. For more money, take the boxes. There is 75¢ in the boxes and 60¢ in the cans.
61. Answers will vary.
62. Answers will vary.
63. B
64. 10 minutes, 1 minute, 2 hours
65. Wednesday
66. Answers will vary.
67. Answers will vary.
68. 12:30, 1:30, 2:00, 3:00, 3:30
69. Answers will vary.
70. December 10, Wednesday
71. No; 8:30 is only $1\frac{1}{2}$ hours after 7:00 *or* 2 hours after 7:00 is 9:00.
72. 10:00
73. 16 children
74. Answers will vary.
75. Answers will vary.
76. 11:30
77. Answers will vary.
78. Miki's vacation is 2 days longer.
79. Sunday; Explanations will vary.
80. Answers will vary.
81. 6, 7, 10, 35
82. Saturday
83. 3:30
84. 8:00, 1:00, 7:00; Answers will vary.
85. July 24
86. 12:00, 30, 1, 5:30
87. 2, 4, 3, 1
88. April 7, June 8; Questions will vary.
89. Stories will vary.
90. 2:00, 2:30, 3:00, 5:00
91. Mara; 14 days; 2 weeks

92. Answers will vary.

93. Answers will vary.

94. Answers will vary.

95. 8:30, 4, 12:30, 2

96. Possible answer: Alike: The hands form a corner (a right angle). The big hands both point to 12. Different: The small hands point to different numbers. The corners (angles) are in different directions.

97. Answers will vary.

98. an hour longer

99. Monday

100. June, November, August